COLLECTED ARTWORKS OF RAOUL KENNEDY
(1970-2010)

ISBN-13: 978-1499590692

ISBN-10: 1499590695

TABLE OF CONTENTS

INTRODUCTION

INTRODUCTION

This collection features thirty-four selected artworks spanning the four decades between 1970 and 2010. They are divided into three sections, of which two sections correspond to themes: *Transitions*, and *Inspiration*. The transitions represent a change in my life, revelation or realization. Inspiration refers to something that inspired me, or that I loved. The primary media for these sections were oil, acrylic, and watercolor pencil. The third section focuses on cartoons and illustrations, some of which also may have involved a transition or inspiration. A sub-category of this section is "Economics through Art" which was an experiment in presenting concepts in economics.

When I first thought about this book, I wasn't sure whether I felt qualified to publish a collection of my works, as I have no formal training in art, apart from a high school art class which I took after I had already begun painting. I feared that I had made numerous blunders from a technical standpoint, whatever they might be.

While compiling this collection a number of questions about art popped up from my "uneducated" standpoint, some possibly nonsensical but nevertheless interesting and perplexing to me.

Is feeling a sense of pride and satisfaction with one's own work enough to validate it as art? Is simply *liking* what you created sufficient? Or perhaps all that matters is that someone *else* can enjoy your work, whether or not you like it yourself.

Apart from the actual efforts we put forward to create something, how much credit should we give to ourselves for any supposed innate talents or abilities we might have? Should some of the credit go to DNA as well? Was I fortunate enough to have received a few genes from one of my ancestors, French painter Antoine Logerot (1777-1844)?

Should the artworks be accompanied by my explanations and interpretations of what I think was happening, or does that spoil the pleasure of art? Should the interpretation of each artwork be entirely left to the viewer?

Is there any single dominant meaning behind an artwork, or are there as many meanings as the number of potential interpretations?

Do my artworks really depict some part of my own reality at the time? Can they help me get to know myself better?

Can artwork have predictive value? Can art help us see into the future or even connect us to the present?

Are our childhood works just as valid as our adult works, or should childhood art be treated as some kind of separate category? If so, artistically speaking, when does childhood start and adulthood begin?

When does art stop becoming art and start becoming more like a textbook? (See the "Economics through Art" section to understand what I'm trying to ask with this question!)

Enough questions --Time to google the answers! I do hope that you will find my art enjoyable, and even informative.

TRANSITIONS

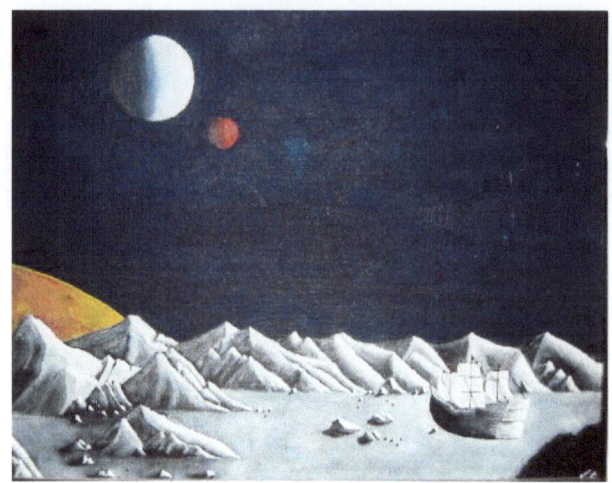

Abandoned Galleon (1976)

Oil on canvas

The stark realization that the last phase of my childhood had ended (represented by the galleon and love of ships) and I was entering a new phase of life.

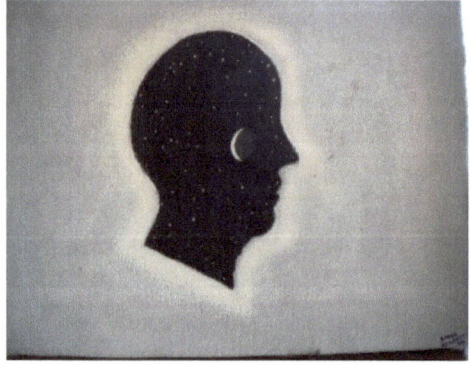

Thought (1979)

Oil on canvas

I had reached a point in my life that required serious reflection about my future.

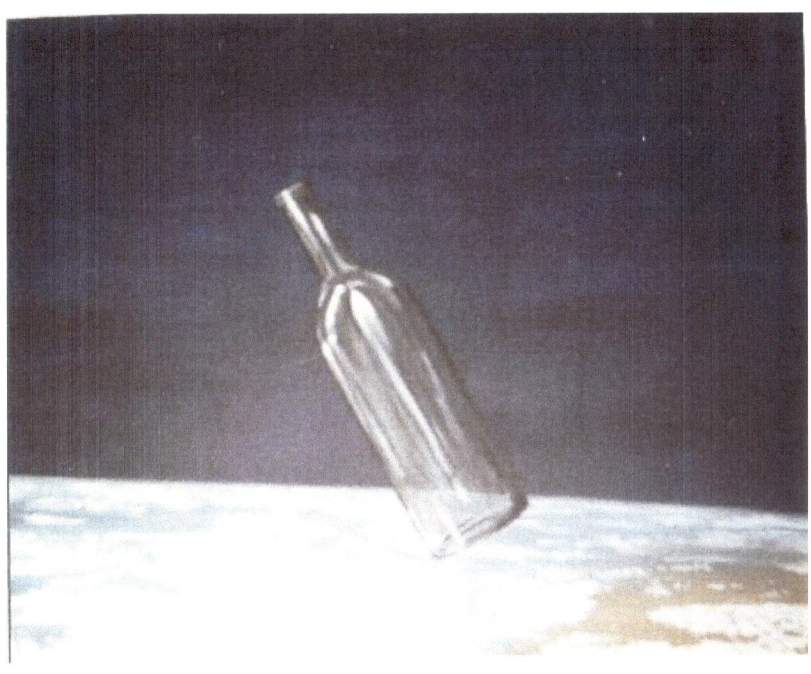

Cultural Indifference (1980)

Oil on canvas

This painting might have been a form of youthful rebellion against the pressures of having to be "cultured" as represented by a bottle of wine (probably a Château Mouton Rothschild)

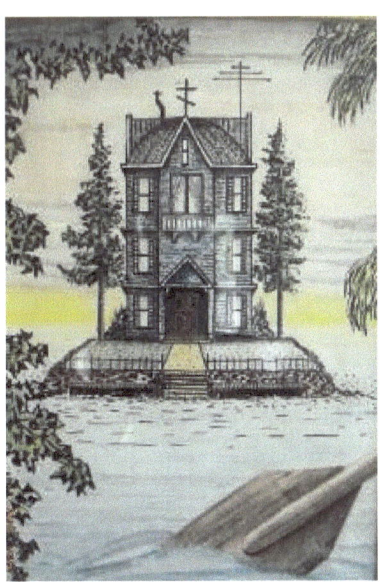

Coming Home (1984)

Watercolor pencil and ink

Symbolically rowing my way back home after having completed my studies.

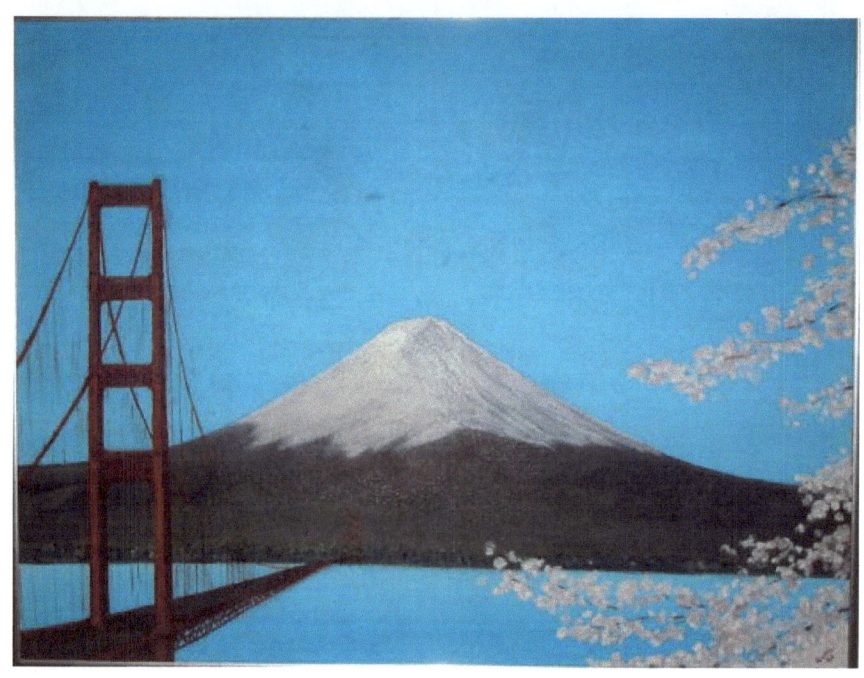

A Golden Gate Bridge to Japan (1986)

Acrylic on canvas

This was inspired by my "link" to my future wife who was in Japan. I was living in San Francisco at the time.

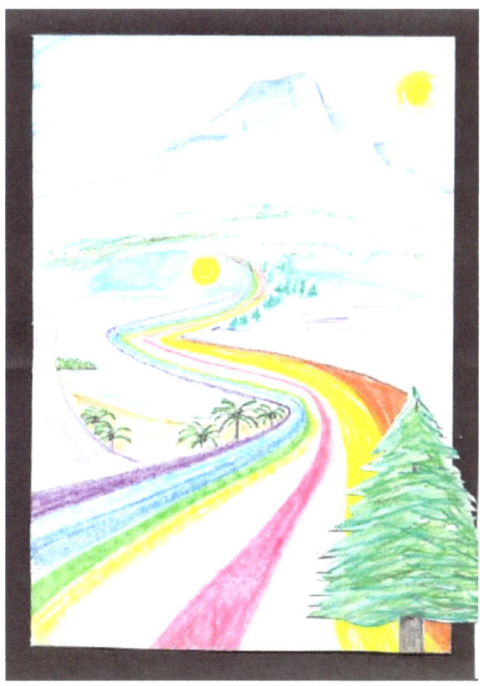

Path to Multi-dimensions (1999)

Watercolor pencil and crayon on paper

My future journey from Japan to Las Vegas, drawn prior to my departure. The mountain in the background may have been influenced by the movie *Close Encounters of the Third Kind* (1977), representing an unknown world ahead. It also reminds me of some of the rock formations and mountains of Red Rock Canyon and environs where I hiked some years later.

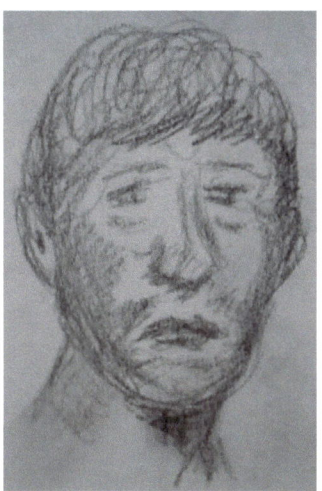

Despair (2005)

Graphite on paper

After being laid off from my job, it became painfully obvious that the economy had fundamentally changed and things weren't going back to the way they were.

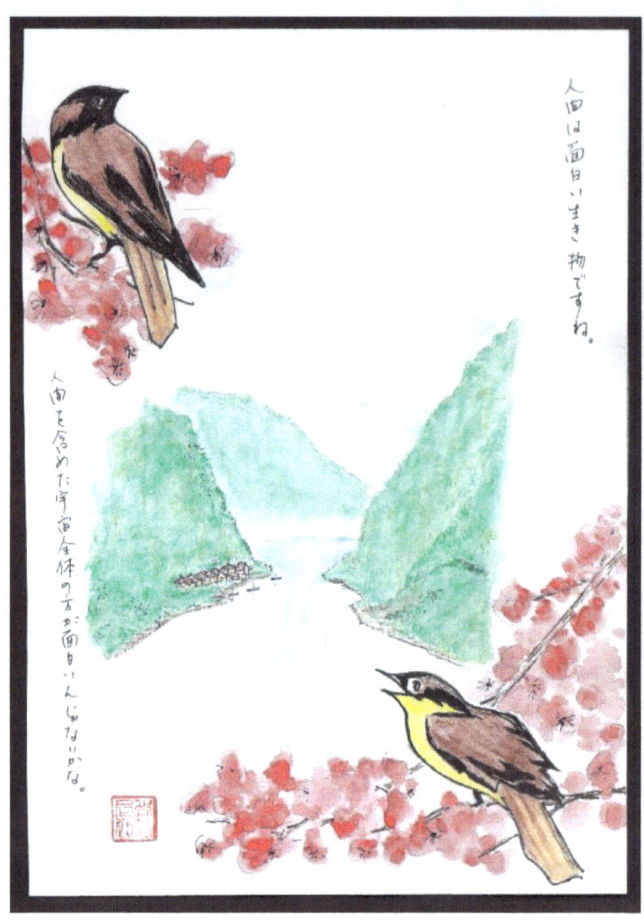

Talking Birds (2006)

Watercolor and ink

I eventually tried to overcome my feelings (see *Despair*), by focusing more on the breathtaking beauty of the natural world around us. The bird on the right says, "*Humans are interesting creatures, aren't they?*" The bird on the left responds, "*But not as interesting as the universe they inhabit.*"(In Japanese)

INSPIRATION

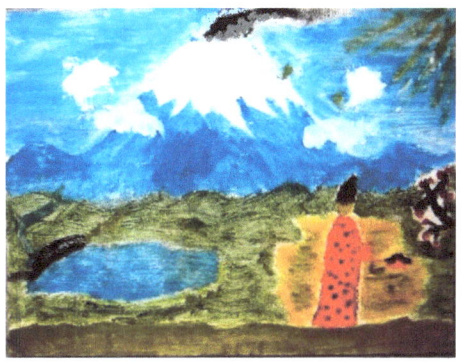

Japan Dreaming (1971)

Oil on canvas

I became attached to Japan early on, unaware of the importance Japan would have on my life many years later. This was my first oil painting, completed after being inspired by a country project on Japan I had done at school.

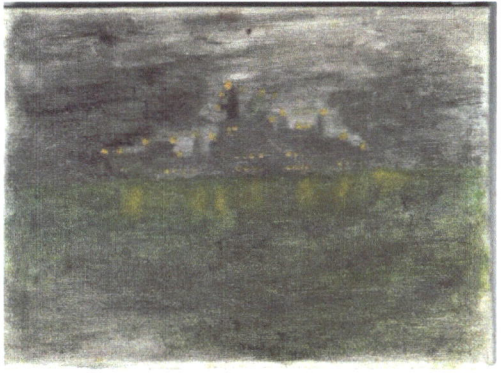

Freighter 1 (1972)

Oil on canvas

This represents my fascination with sea vessels including galleons and old rusty freighters (preferably shrouded in mist and traveling through murky waters). From my desk with a remarkable view of Sydney harbor I loved watching the ships and would not only draw them but also recorded their departure and/or arrival times so I could see them again.

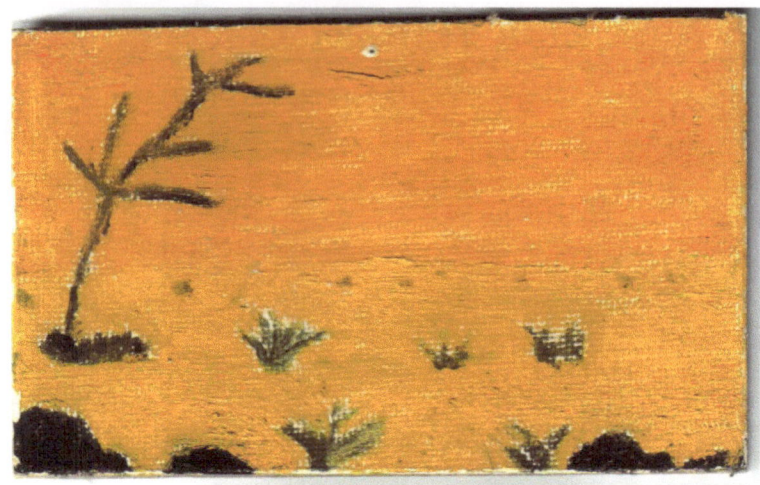

Desert (1972)

Oil on canvas

Inspired by travels through Australia's outback in the summer of 1972.

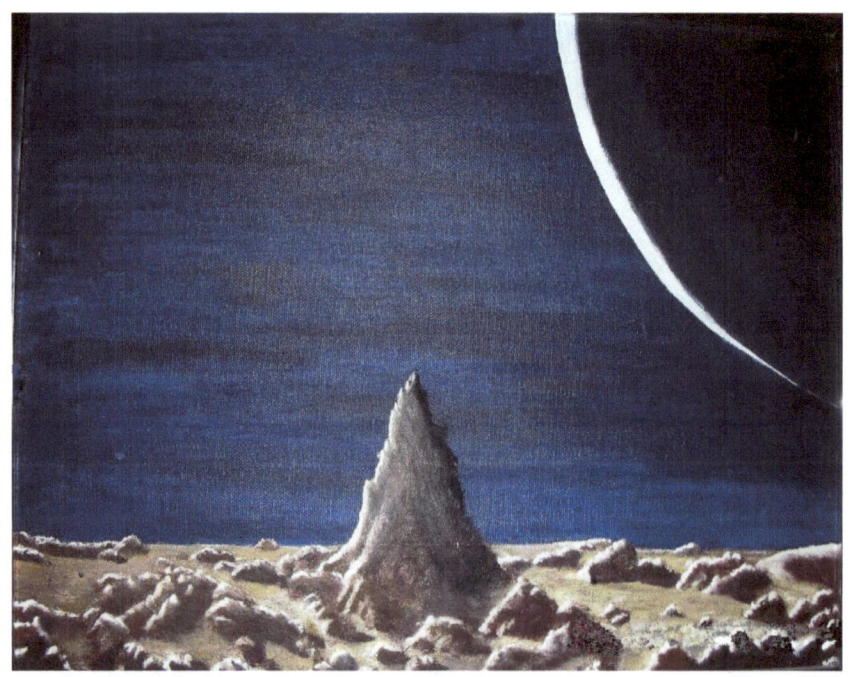

Cosmic Ego (1978)

Oil on canvas

By this time I was more firmly established in a new world (my school).

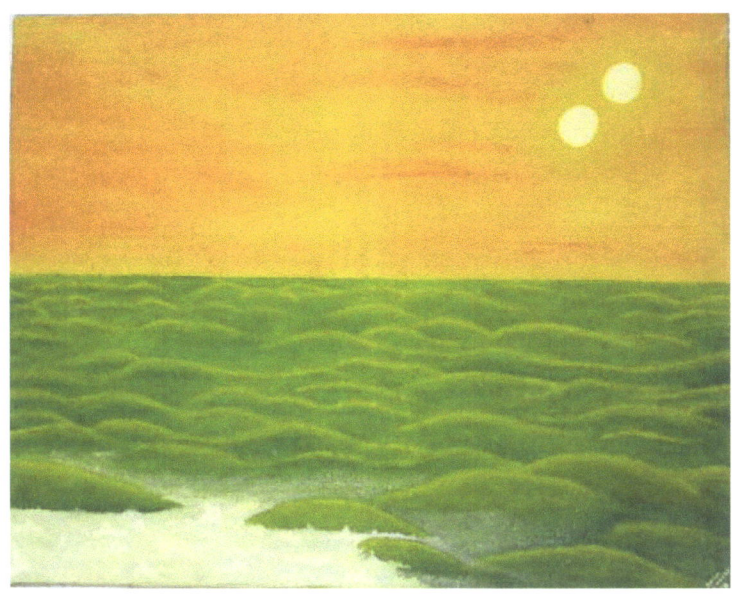

Twin suns (1978)

Oil on canvas

A planet in another universe that had two suns. The fog was reminiscent of the fog that rolls into the San Francisco Bay Area.

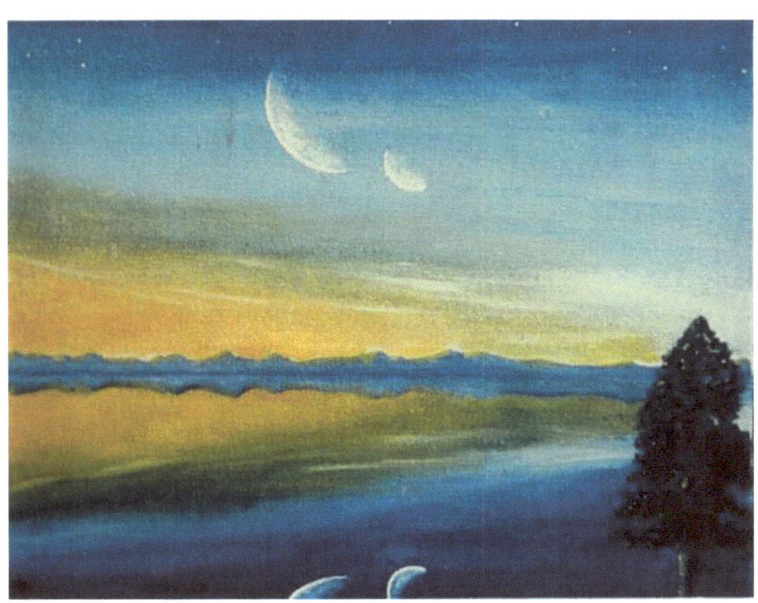

Para-Earth (1978)

Oil on canvas

An earth-like world with two moons.

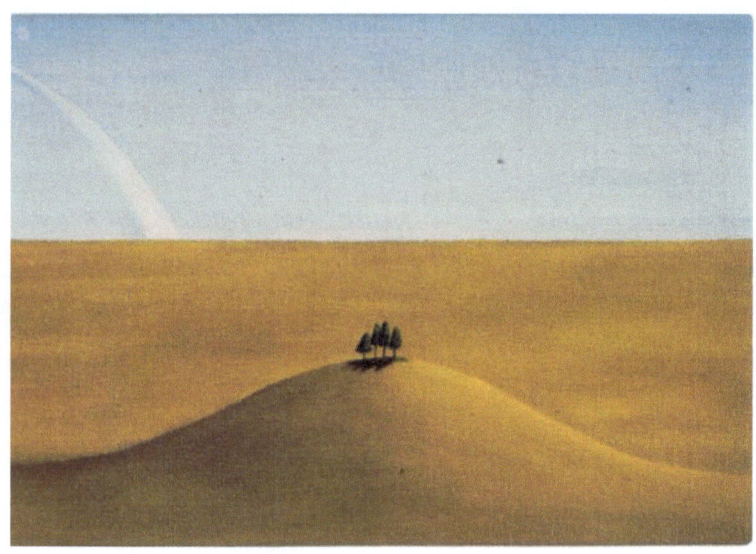

Family Bosom (1978)

Oil on canvas

The four trees on the "bosom" hill represent our family members and the closeness I felt to them.

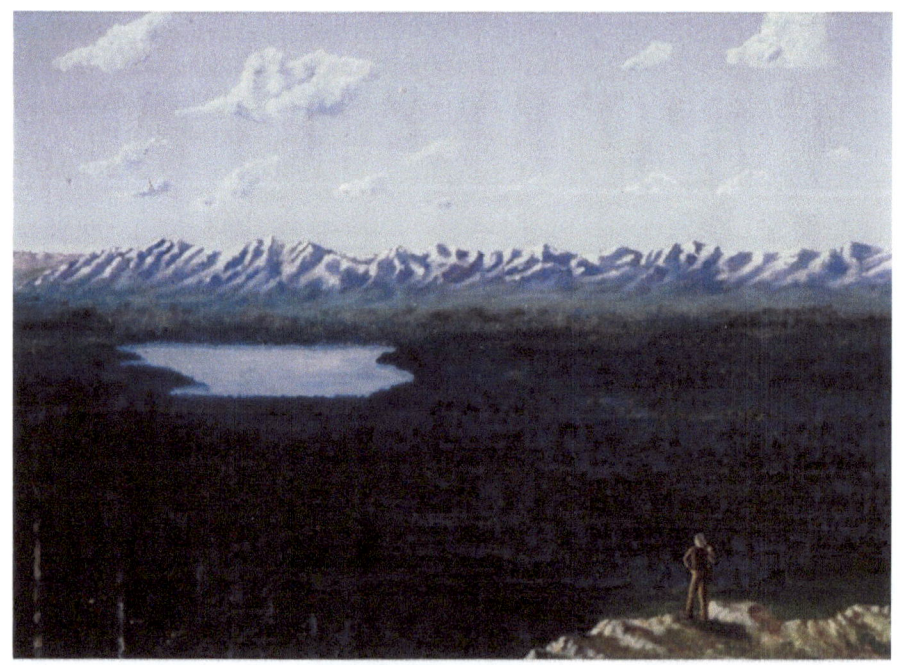

Proud Pioneer (1979)

Oil on canvas

Undoubtedly inspired by living and working in Alaska that summer.

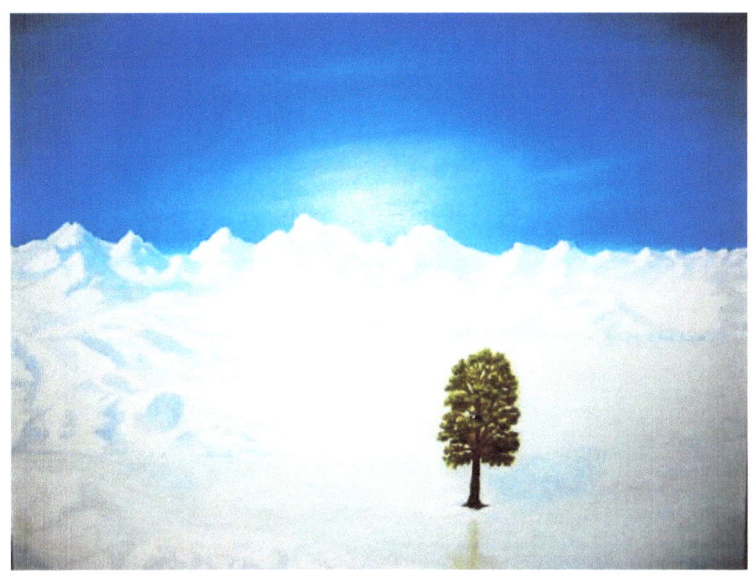

Antarctic Wilderness (1979)

Oil on canvas

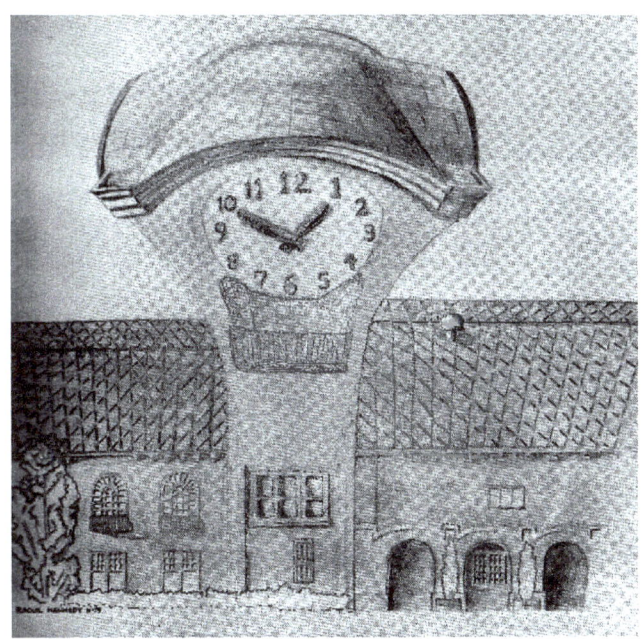

Clock Tower Distortion (1979)

Graphite on paper

Inspired by M.C. Escher, this the clock tower of Tamalpais High School in California.

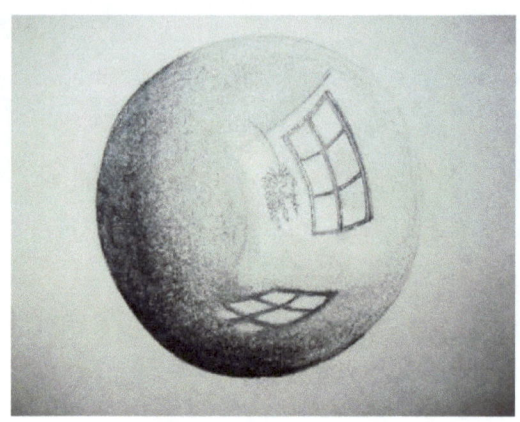

Water Droplet (1979)

Graphite on paper

Also likely inspired by M.C. Escher.

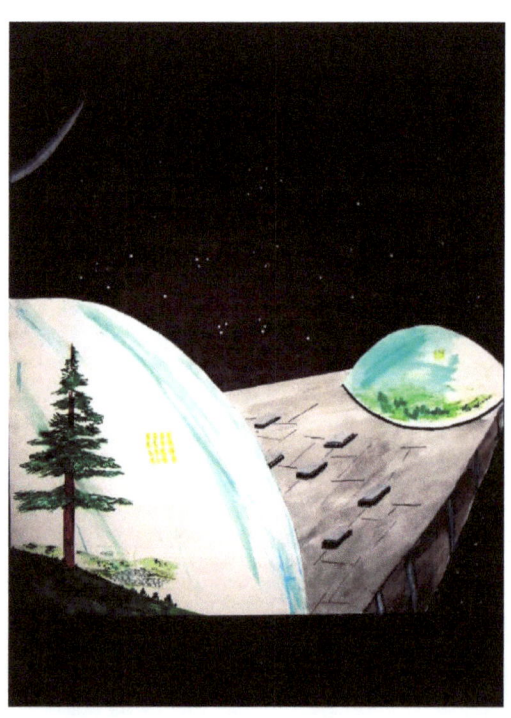

Home (1979)

Watercolor and pen on paper

I dreamed of a world where we would be able to live in space colonies (space condos?). The bubbles are bio-domes. Probably influenced by the movie *Silent Running* (1972).

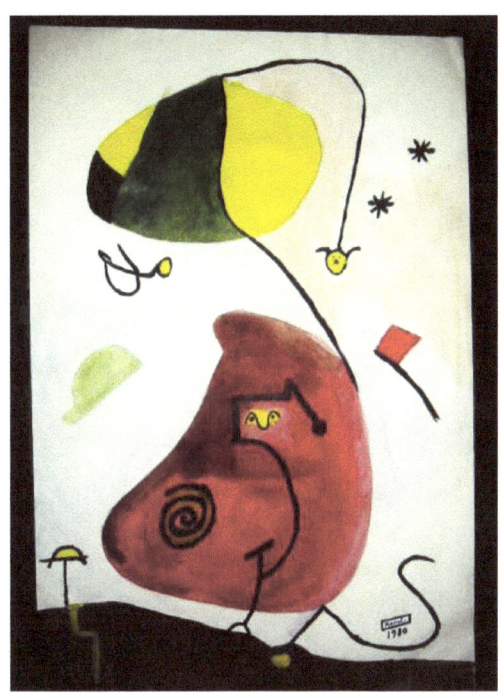

Homage to Miró (1980)

Watercolor and pen on paper

Referring to the famous artist Joan Miró i Ferrà.

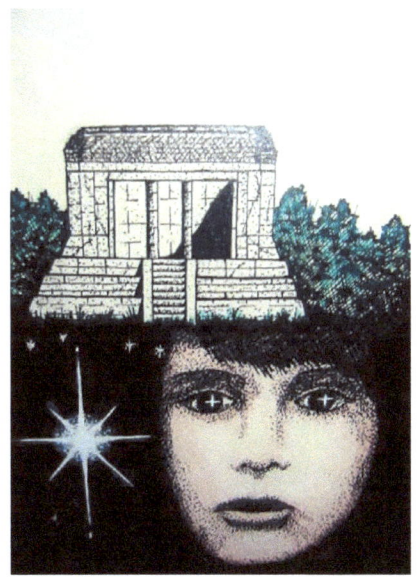

Maya I (1980)

Watercolor pencil and pen on paper

My future daughter was named Maya (born nine years after this picture). She agrees that the image of the girl here resembles her somewhat!

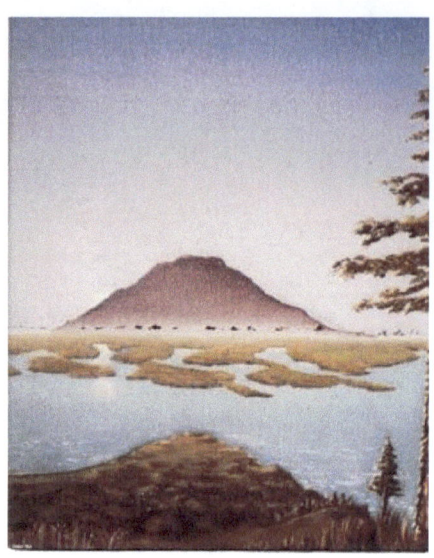

Untitled (1980)

Oil on canvas

A gift for my mother on her birthday. Thirty-two years later in 2012, while looking out to the sea from Churaumi Aquarium in Okinawa, Japan I was reminded of the painting and snapped a photo (below), although the island in the background appears small.

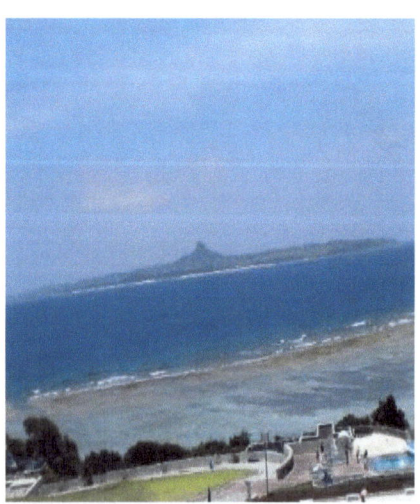

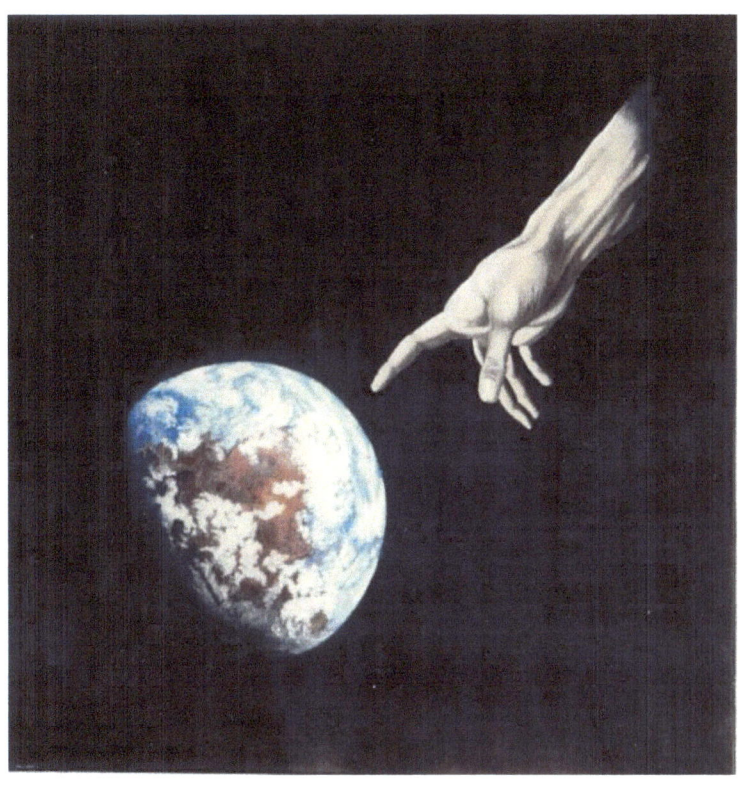

Creation: Part II (1980)

Oil on canvas

I named this painting *Part II* although no *Part I* preceded it. I suppose that *Childbirth*, painted four years later, could have been the Part I. I also pondered the possibility that the "true" Part I may be impossible to represent since prior to Planck time (roughly 10^{-43} seconds), the laws of physics, as currently understood, break down.

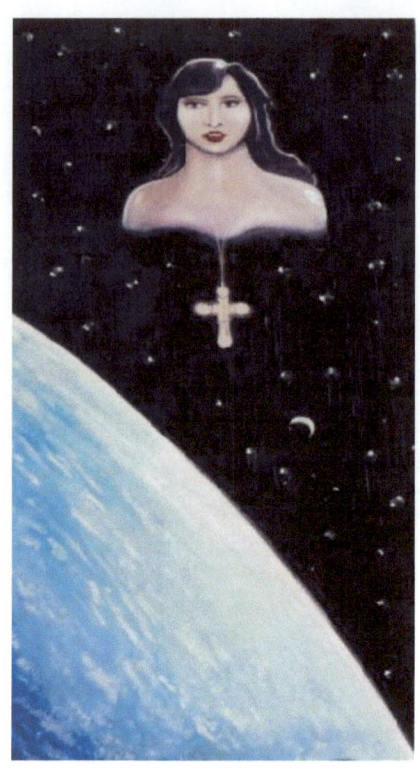

Maya II (1984)

Acrylic and oil on canvas

Painted one year before I met my future wife. (Also see Maya I (1980))

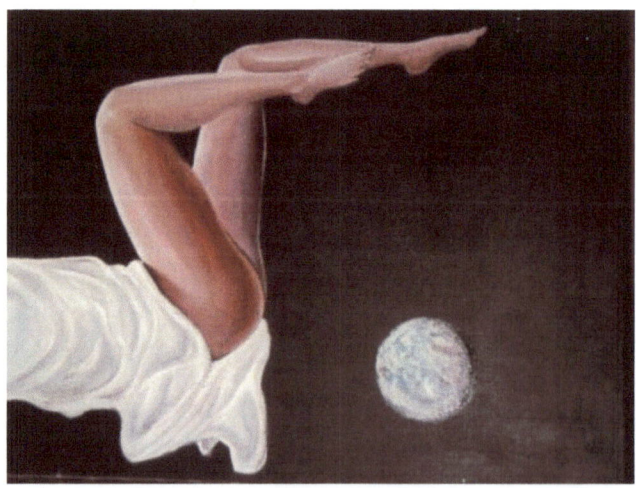

Childbirth (1984)

Acrylic and oil on canvas

Earth is born. Could be the Part I to *Creation: Part II* (1980).

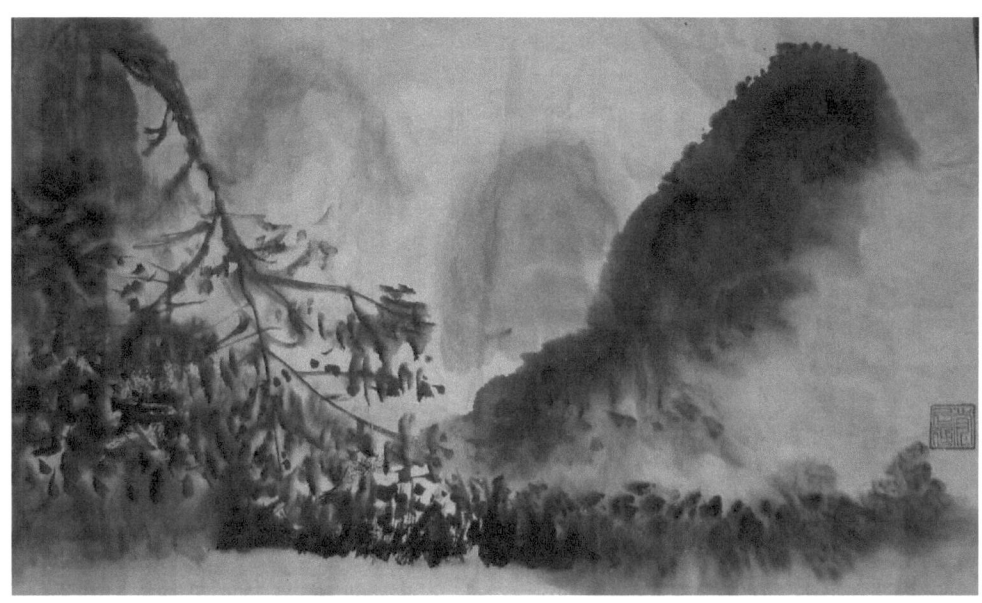

Imagining Taroko (2008)

Black ink on paper

I became interested in Chinese ink paintings in 2008 and wanted to return to Taiwan after having made previous trips in the 1990's. *Taroko* referred to Taiwan's Taroko National Park, which I later visited in 2012 and again in 2013.

In 2013, landslides were reported by *Liberty Times Net*. A photo of the area appears in an article at: http://news.ltn.com.tw/news/life/paper/676799

CARTOONS, ILLUSTRATIONS AND OTHER

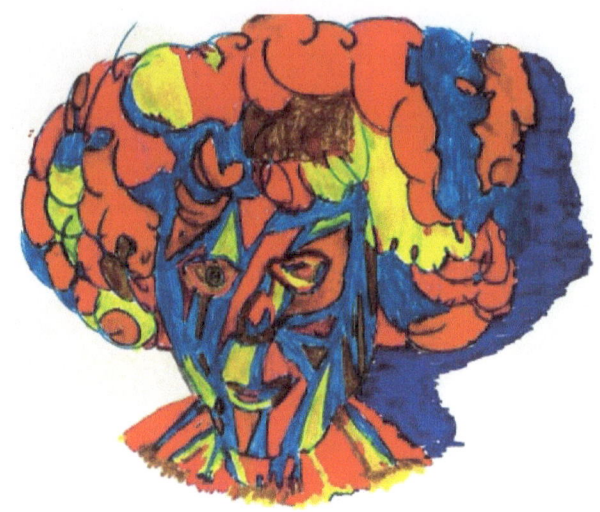

Artistic Resolution (1971)

Magic marker on paper

Likely inspired by the rock musical *Hair*, and Jimi Hendrix. I also think that this drawing represents a resolution to pursue art more seriously. Following this, I began to experiment with painting in oil.

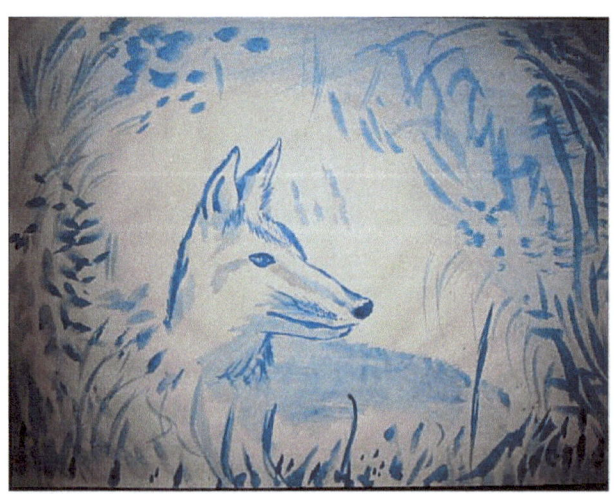

Study in Colored Ink (1980)

Colored ink on paper

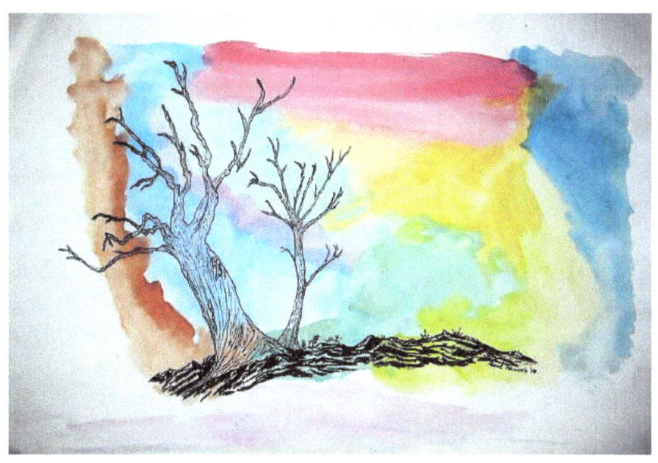

Study in Watercolor and Ink (1980)

Watercolor and ink on paper

A number of works were done while I was employed as an illustrator at University of California, Davis (UC Davis), and unfortunately they cannot be reproduced here. I titled some of my favorites as follows: Agricultural Practices (1981), Engineering (1981), Physics (1981), Physiology (1981), Tribute to UC Davis (1981), Casual Pose (1981) and they are also listed in the Table of Contents.

DWEEFUS THE LENDER by R.K.

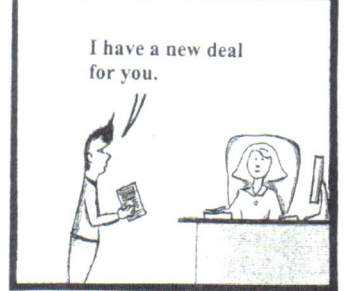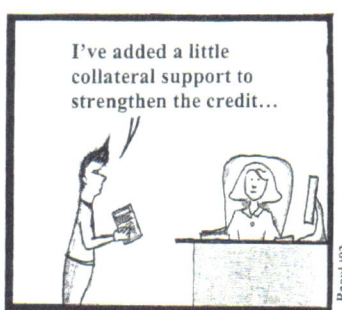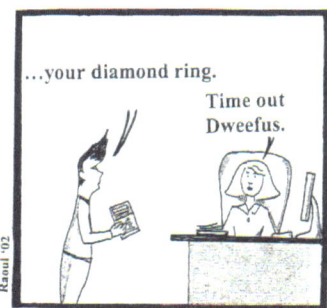

Commercial Banking (2001)

Ink on paper

This cartoon was a gift to my supervisor at a lending office of a bank. The lender tries to get a weak loan request go through easier with his supervisor's ring used as collateral.

ECONOMICS THROUGH ART

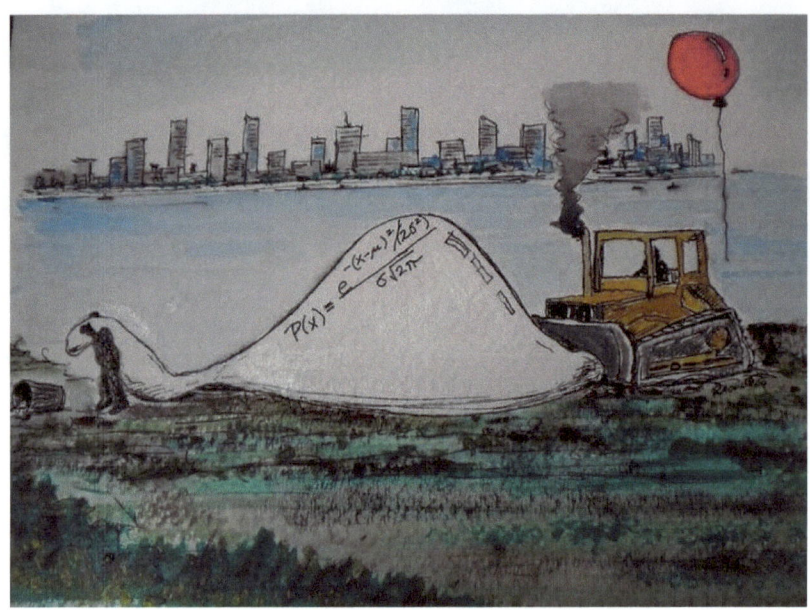

Goodbye Gauss (2009)

Watercolor and ink

This was a first attempt at conveying concepts in economics through art. After pondering books by Nassim Nicholas Taleb (*Fooled by Randomness* and *The Black Swan*) I realized that the Gaussian "normal" distribution was most likely a questionable foundation for financial economics. Here, the poor normal distribution, marked with the equation describing it, is unceremoniously taken out to the dump, and in the process is being distorted, with a fat (or goofy?) left tail and a squashed right tail.

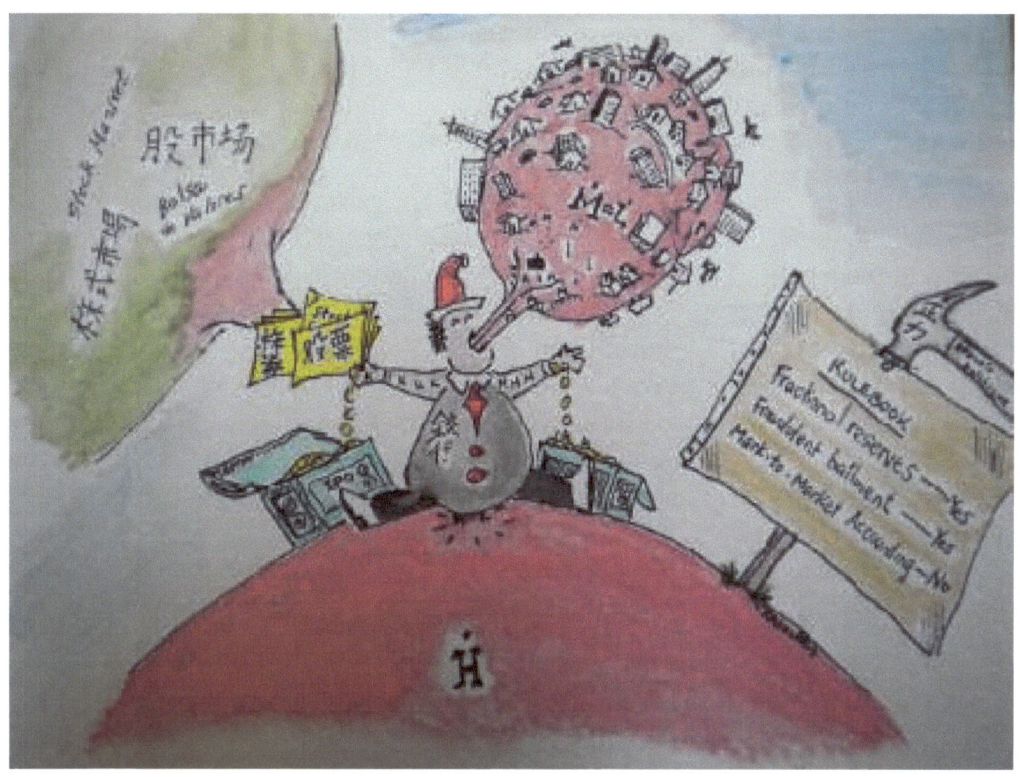

Monetary System Theory (2009)

Watercolor and ink on paper

This was also an attempt to convey economics through art. Here I hoped to illustrate our monetary and banking system. This project was more of a challenge than I had expected and perhaps tests the boundaries of what is tolerable in art (!?).

This drawing depicts an IPO (initial public offering). Although the idea initially came from a *bank* IPO, the logic could apply to other enterprises as well. The pink base upon which the banker sits is central bank "base money" "H" (also called "high powered money) upon which the bankers can lend under fractional reserve rules (see the law "rulebook" at right , hammered in by political power). The banker literally "spits" out money "M" the bank has legally created through the process of lending (credit creation), which in our debt-money system, also represents a liability "L" (M=L). The objects floating in the bubble above him are assets that the banker lends upon, helping to contribute to asset inflation and bubbles in various sectors. The stock market, represented by the huge bubble on the left, is also one of the asset markets that can be inflated by the new money creation. New IPO shares are issued (the letter "K" on the banker's arm represents capital of the enterprise to be turned into public shares) and sold to the investing public for cash which accumulates in the left-hand coffer of the company owners. If the company relies on bank financing, new money is created ("M" on the bankers' arm) and that cash drops into the coffer on the right (representing the accounts of those who received the proceeds of the financing). The rulebook on the right posits some fundamental problems with the banking system : 1. Fractional reserves (for example, banks can legally lend out $10 for every $1 of deposits – literally multiplying their reserves and creating money out of thin air) 2. Fraudulent bailment (depositor money is supposedly being held in storage by the bank, but in fact the law permits the money to be lent out within certain limits, so much of the money isn't available) 3. Mark-to-market accounting: "No" because banks do not usually wish to report the value of their loan portfolios at market value – otherwise losses and insolvency would be far more obvious. A central bank is also integral to the current monetary system, and is partly shown through the "base money" H (at the bottom of the picture) which appears on the central bank's balance sheet.

Although the focus is the Initial Public Offering (IPO), the cartoon is not a criticism of IPOs. The IPO is used to help illustrate its context within the wider monetary framework. The major concern is that the current monetary system can contribute to inflation in asset (and other prices) causing major instability in markets leading to subsequent crashes, as well as distortions in the distribution of wealth from money-printing. A related and critical issue is the centralized control of interest and exchange rates. Knowing in advance what central banks are going to do with regards to exchange rates and bond market interventions/tapers gives a remarkable edge to those privy to the information to accumulate wealth (both from capital gains as well as well-timed shorts in down markets) --beyond what uncontrolled markets could produce. If certain parties are benefiting from consistent gains (and able to dodge volatility with uncanny ability), then the possibility of some form of *information asymmetry* has to be looked at: More specifically, the control and selective dissemination of very valuable information at the central bank and other policy-making levels.

The "dot" above the H, M and L is the symbol for "growth of." The color pink represents printed/created money. (In English, French, Chinese, Japanese and Spanish).

INCOMPLETE AND MISSING WORKS

There are a number of works that have gone missing, or are not featured in this collection.

I opted not to sell my artworks with only one exception, *Spaceship* (1977). The buyer was a retiring teacher who loved science fiction. Since it had special meaning for him, I felt good about selling it to him. I heard that in his last years of teaching he kept the painting on his classroom wall.

A painting that I was unable to add to this collection was *Meandering* (1979), which features two tiny single-passenger spaceships "cruising" through space with a huge planet (or moon) looming in the background. Other artworks included Tam High Perspective (1977), Incomplete Sphere (1979), Nature Wild (1980), and Frozen Shiitake (1999), and a few Christmas themed illustrations, among others. The "Economics through Art" series which I experimented with in 2009 was more difficult than I had expected and I began to wonder whether I was departing from the world of art and into something more of a "headache"!

Some paintings I did not complete due to other priorities or eventual lack of interest. One concept which I had some 30 years ago I still hope to put into an artwork. As for the future, I hope that other ideas will come to me--most likely when I least expect them! Along the way the road might be a bit snow-bound, though…

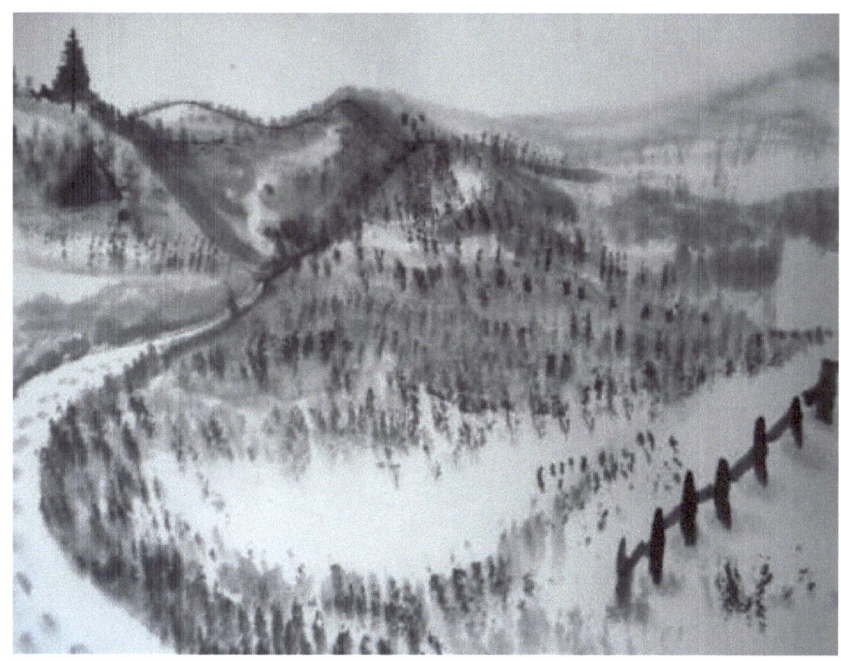

Snowy Road (2010)

Black ink on paper